Grolier
Album
Series

# ALBUM OF UPPER CANADA

**Wesley B. Turner**

Grolier Limited
TORONTO

# Contents

Copyright © 1987 by Grolier Limited. All rights reserved.

**Canadian Cataloguing in Publication Data**

Turner, Wesley B. 1933–
    Album of  Upper Canada

(Grolier album series)

ISBN 0-7172-1868-6

1. Frontier and pioneer life — Ontario — Juvenile literature.
2. Ontario — History — 1791-1841 — Juvenile literature.*
3. Ontario — Social conditions — To 1867 — Juvenile literature.*
I. Title. II. Series.

FC3071.T87 1987              j971.3′02              C87-094170-4

1234567890              DWF              6543210987

Printed and bound in Canada

# Introduction

Upper Canada was both a place and a time. Geographically, it was the British colony that extended from the junction of the St. Lawrence and Ottawa Rivers, westward along the northern edge of the Great Lakes. Chronologically, Upper Canada extended from the last decade of the eighteenth century into the middle decade of the nineteenth.

In this album you will look at the creation of Upper Canada as a separate colony in 1791, at the political and military events of the next half century, and at the reunion of Upper Canada and Lower Canada in 1841. This album will introduce you to the various groups of people who came to populate the colony: first Loyalists, then American settlers, and still later large numbers of immigrants from the British isles. Along the shores of the upper St. Lawrence River, Lake Ontario and Lake Erie, this small pioneer society took shape as roads, towns, and farms were carved out of the wilderness. It was a society that became the basis of the present-day province of Ontario. The *Album of Upper Canada* will give you a glimpse of the economy, culture, religion and education of that society.

Some of the buildings, artifacts and documents pictured in this album still exist. If you visit historic sites and museums in Ontario, you can see them for yourself. In doing so, you can better understand and enjoy one of the most important periods in Canadian history.

# The Establishment of Upper Canada

The land known as Upper Canada had been a home for native peoples long before Europeans settled in it or gave it that name. These early inhabitants included the Neutrals in the Niagara Peninsula, Hurons around Georgian Bay and several Algonkian tribes farther north. By the end of the eighteenth century, their numbers had decreased so that only a few thousand continued to live in Upper Canada. The arrival of increasing numbers of new settlers to the area meant that permanent changes to the landscape and to the lifestyle of the early inhabitants were inevitable.

By 1784, approximately 6000 United Empire Loyalists had settled in the colony of Quebec. As a result the English population in the colony grew substantially. Quebec was predominantly French—its laws were French and its land system was seigneurial. The new English settlers were unfamiliar and uncomfortable with the French laws and land system and began requesting something more familiar—English laws and a freehold system of land tenure that would allow them to own their land.

The British government passed the Constitutional or Canada Act in 1791. This Act divided the colony of Quebec into Upper and Lower Canada. Upper Canada was up the St. Lawrence River, west of its junction with the Ottawa River. Most of the English-speaking population in the colony lived there, and the division allowed them to have their requested laws and land system.

Between 1791 and 1841, Upper Canada grew quickly. Population increased from approximately 25 000 in 1791 to approximately 400 000 in 1838. Villages and towns were established to meet the needs of large numbers of immigrants from the United States and Britain.

By 1841, many changes had taken place in Upper Canada. It had grown from a pioneer community into a complex society poised to enter the modern age.

A large number of Pennsylvania German families made the trip to Upper Canada in Conestoga wagons. These wagons were well suited to travel on early roads and could also ford streams fairly easily. Because of their large capacity, they were most useful in transporting the large loads early settlers brought with them.

The Toronto Purchase. This artist's fanciful rendition of the Toronto Purchase portrays the meeting between Lord Dorchester, Governor of Canada and the invited chiefs of the Mississauga Indians aboard HMS *Seneca* in 1788. The purpose of the meeting was to gain control of the site on Lake Ontario.

The shaded area on this map of present-day Canada represents Upper Canada, 1791-1841.

**Population Graph 1791–1840**

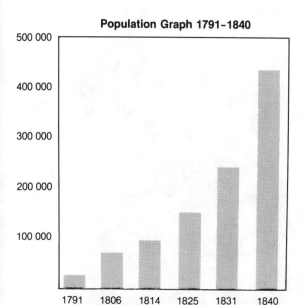

The population of Upper Canada grew quickly between 1791 and 1841. Although there are no exact population statistics for that period—no census was ever done between 1791 and 1841—these figures illustrate the rate at which the population of Upper Canada grew. In fact, between 1831 and 1841, the population almost doubled.

**FOR DISCOVERY**
1. Who were the Loyalists?
2. Why did the British Government divide the colony of Quebec in 1791?
3. Draw a graph that shows the population growth for your province since 1900. Use ten-year intervals, starting with census year 1901. Your local library or Statistics Canada can provide the information you need.

Loyalist encampment on the Bay of Quinte. United Empire Loyalists left the United States to settle in British North America as early as 1776, but the majority came in 1783 and 1784. They left because they did not support the American War of Independence against Britain. Many came to Canada with few possessions. The government gave them land, tools and seed to start farming. Later, money was granted as compensation for what they had lost in the United States. About 6000 Loyalists settled along the St. Lawrence River west of Montreal, from present-day Cornwall to Brockville, and at the western end of Lake Ontario.

# Where People Came From — Early Settlement in the Wilderness

The earliest European settlers in Upper Canada were French people who came up the St. Lawrence River. After 1783, their numbers were overwhelmed by the large migration of Loyalists from the United States. Most came from the states of New York and Pennsylvania, travelling on foot, horseback, or if they were fortunate, in covered wagons. Among these refugees were the Loyalist Mohawks who were led by chief Joseph Brant. They settled in the area along the Grand River.

Soon other Americans, not refugees, began to head for Upper Canada. They had heard about its fertile lands and about Lieutenant-Governor Simcoe's promise of generous grants. This movement continued after Simcoe's time. According to an account of 1807:

> Families from the United States are daily coming into the province, bringing with them their stock and utensils of husbandry, in order to establish themselves on new lands, invited by the exuberance [fertility] of the soil, the mildness of the government, and an almost total exemption from taxes. These people either purchase lands from the British subjects, to whom they have been granted, or take them upon lease . . . . Many farmers from the neighbouring states, who are wealthy, procure grants of their own . . . .

Upper Canada had a varied and mixed population from its outset. Immigrants from the British Isles came in only small numbers until after the War of 1812 (1815). Then they came in thousands every year and scattered across all of Upper Canada.

In 1791 John Graves Simcoe was appointed the first Lieutenant-Governor of Upper Canada. Some of Simcoe's policies were far-sighted. He tried to open Upper Canada by building roads and by encouraging immigration through generous land grants.

Joseph Brant was a principal chief of the Six Nations Indians. During the American War of Independence he and his Mohawks fought on the side of the British. After the war, they moved to the valley of the Grand River, where Brant was given a large tract of land. While continuing to act as leader of his people, Brant did missionary work, wrote several religious books, and translated into Mohawk parts of the Gospels and the Church of England prayer book. He died in November 1807.

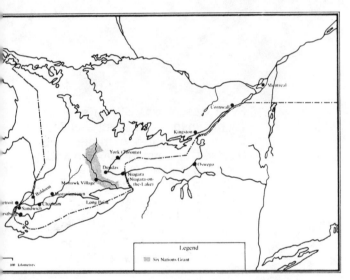

Upper Canada was very sparsely populated in 1805.

The Loyalists were people "of no trade and all trades, of all grades of wealth, education and social position ... who through loyalty, religion, interest or influence disapproved of independence .... They were not conspicuous for wealth, social influence, office, professional prominence, or active hostility."

The "Berczy Settlers" were a group of Germans who came to Upper Canada in 1794. Originally they had been recruited by William Berczy from various German states for a land settlement scheme in upper New York. When this proved unsuccessful, Berczy began negotiating with Governor Simcoe, and eventually he received 26 000 hectares of land in what would become Markham. The property shown here was originally deeded by the Crown to Peter Stiver, a "Berczy settler," in 1803. The early log home can be seen behind the house.

8

Some immigrants preferred to live in groups thus providing support and help for each other in the new land. These included Scottish Roman Catholics from Glengarry who tended to head for Glengarry County where kinfolk lived, as well as the Irish, the Germans, the Pennsylvania Dutch and religious groups like the Amish and Quakers.

At that time, the only way to cross the Atlantic was by sailing ship. It was not a comfortable or safe voyage as this account from 1807 shows:

> On the 13th of June, about eleven o'clock in the forenoon, we sailed out of Cork Harbour, [Ireland] . . . . The weather, for the first eight or ten days . . . was so extremely unpleasant, and the winds so very unfavourable that we made but little progress. After that time, the weather became milder and more agreeable . . . . On the 27th of July, we anchored before the city of Quebec, after a voyage of 43 days and a half. During this short period, twelve of our party were consigned to a watery grave; and we interred as many more in different islands of the St. Lawrence. All them were children under fourteen years of age.

Nevertheless, the tolerance of peoples with different languages and customs, combined with attractions of land and economic opportunity, continued to attract many immigrants from Britain and Europe.

Peter Reesor was one of several young men from Pennsylvania Dutch (an English corruption of *Deutsch,* or German) families who came to Upper Canada in the 1790s to explore the area as a possible site for relocation. After trading his horse for land in Whitchurch, Markham Township, Reesor walked back to Pennsylvania. The family came to Markham in 1804.

This stone house built by Peter Reesor in 1831 was typical of Pennsylvania Dutch architecture. The people in the photograph are descendants of the original Pennsylvania Dutch settlers in Markham.

In 1803 Thomas Talbot received a land grant of 5000 acres (2000 hectares) for a settlement he was to promote. By 1812, he had placed only thirty families. His main success came after the War of 1812, and by 1836, Talbot had 28 townships under his supervision and had settled about forty thousand people.

## FOR DISCOVERY

1. Why did some immigrants to Upper Canada prefer to come and settle in groups?
2. Imagine that you are a Loyalist getting ready to flee to Upper Canada. Write a short dialogue that might take place as you and your family decide what to take with you and what you have to leave behind.
3. If you had been a poor farmer living in Britain around 1815, would you have been willing to travel to the colony and settle there? Why or why not?

Companies were formed to promote settlement. The most important of these was the Canada Company, which was founded in 1825. In return for a large payment to the provincial government, the Canada Company received more than 400 000 hectares of Crown Reserves and the Huron Tract, a total of more than 800 000 hectares of land. The company quickly began ambitious programmes of road-building, school-building and public works to attract settlers. By the time its contract with the government ended in 1843 it had played a major role in colonizing the western part of Upper Canada.

Living conditions on board immigrant ships were far from comfortable. There was often extreme overcrowding and immigrants endured their trip below deck in cramped bunks with poor food and little fresh air.

# Clearing Land, Farming

Immigrants could buy or lease land although some were given land by the government. These included the Loyalists, soldiers leaving the army and poor people sent to Upper Canada by the British government.

A new settler had plenty to do to establish a farm from which to make a living. Most of Upper Canada was forested, which meant that trees had to be cut down and their stumps removed before the land could be properly cultivated. Chopping down trees with an axe and cutting them up with a handsaw was difficult, slow work.

Some of the felled trees were used to build log cabins and furniture and to make tools, but most were burned. The ashes were then carefully collected and used to make soap or sold as potash to merchants.

That left the problem of the stumps. Even with the help of animals, they were extremely difficult to dig out, so they were usually left to rot for a few years. Meanwhile, crops were grown in the spaces between and around them. Rocks and brush that were removed as the land was cleared were often used to build fences.

The earliest settlers had only the simplest of farm implements and many tasks had to be done painstakingly by hand. Farm animals were at first very scarce and were, in any case, of limited use in the stump-dotted fields. The situation gradually improved, but for many years the life of most pioneer farmers was one of back-breaking dawn-to-dusk labour.

Wheat and corn were the main crops, and barley, oats and potatoes might also be cultivated on a smaller scale. Most farmers raised vegetables as well for their own use, and perhaps some for sale, and kept some livestock, especially pigs and cows. Some farmers, however, soon began specializing—particularly in the Niagara Peninsula, where the milder weather was well suited to fruit-growing. Wild plants, berries and nuts were gathered to supplement cultivated crops.

The early farms were messy-looking, but many were very productive because much of the land, fed by thousands of years of leaf mould, was extremely rich. The settlers quickly learned to judge a piece of land by the kinds of trees that grew on it. The presence of walnut, cherry, hickory and basswood indicated soil of the highest quality. On the other hand, cedar, pine and hemlock land was, in the words of one settler, "hardly worth accepting as a present."

Before settlers could obtain legal title to the land, they had to fulfill certain requirements. "They must within the term of two years clear fit for cultivation and fence, ten acres [4 ha] of the lot obtained; build a house 16 by 20 feet [5 by 6 metres] of logs or frame, with a shingle roof; also cut down all timber in front of and the whole width of the lot...33 feet [10 metres] of which must be cleared smooth and left for half the public road."

Council-Office, Dec. 29, 1798.

# YONGE-STREET.

NOTICE is hereby given to all persons settled, or about to settle on
*YONGE-STREET*, and whose *locations*
have not yet been confirmed by order of
the PRESIDENT in council, that before such
locations can be confirmed it will be expected that the following CONDITIONS
be complied with :

*First.* That within *twelve months* from the
time they are permitted to occupy
their respective lots, they do cause
to be erected thereon a good and
sufficient dwelling house, of at least
16 feet by 20 in the clear, and do
occupy the same in *Person*, or by a
substantial *Tenant.*

*Second,* THAT within the same period of
time, they do clear and fence *five*
acres, of their respective lots, in a
substantial manner.

*Third,* THAT within the same period of
time, they do open as much of the
Yonge-Street road as lies between
the front of their lots and the middle of said road, amounting to one
acre or thereabouts.

*JOHN SMALL,* C. E. C.

Settlers on Yonge Street had
several conditions to fulfill
within one year of receiving
land.

The task of clearing land for public roads was a
difficult one and if not supervised, it was often
left undone.

Even with hard work and care, the pioneer farmers of Upper Canada could not be sure of a large crop or good prices for what they produced. Bad weather, diseases and insects could all damage the crops, and there was little farmers could do about them. They could only hope that they would harvest their crop before disaster struck. A few, if they could afford it, switched from an unsuccessful crop to a more promising one. It was a hard life. Unless the farmer lived near an urban centre, it was also very lonely.

The task of clearing the land was indeed enormous. Oxen were used to haul the timber from the forest and to provide the power to remove the stumps that remained after the huge trees had been felled. Once the fields began to take shape, oxen were yoked to wooden ploughs and harrows.

Potash was usually a farmer's first profitable "crop." After felled trees were burned, the men would leach the lye from the ash by pouring water over it. The women then boiled the residue, stirring often until the mixture turned dark red. The process was tedious and it could take a whole week to produce one barrel of potash.

People were concerned with the most basic need—food. In order to meet that need, their farms had to produce enough crops. After a crop had been grown for several years, the soil would lose its nutrients and the crops would dwindle. As long as there remained plenty of available land, many pioneer families simply abandoned their original land once it was worn out and sought new locations. Some, however, even in these early days, followed more careful methods of farming. They maintained the soil's fertility by rotating crops or by allowing a piece of land to lie fallow, or unused, for a few years. This allowed the soil to regain its nutrients.

## FOR DISCOVERY

1. What were the main crops cultivated by farmers in Upper Canada?
2. You have just arrived in Upper Canada and have chosen a site for your new home. Make a list of the things you must do in order to obtain title to your land. Include materials you will need and how much time you feel each task will take.
3. List the problems faced by pioneer farmers. Do farmers today still face any of these problems?

Improvements in agricultural methods gradually made the planting, cultivating and harvesting of crops easier. Horse power was an improvement many farmers took advantage of as soon as they could.

Winnowing, or separating grain from the chaff, was done in the barn. The doors were left open to create a draft, and the mixture of chaff and grain was tossed into the air from a blanket. The wind blew the lighter chaff away.

# Transportation

Efficient transportation was a necessity for Upper Canada, whose farmers depended on trade to make a living. Lieutenant-Governor Simcoe realized this and started work on major roads such as Yonge Street and Dundas Street.

When settlers arrived, one of the conditions on which they were granted land was that they clear a roadway in front of their farms. In fact, few settlers bothered, and most roads were merely tracks through the woods. They were uncomfortable to travel on even under the best conditions. In the spring or summer or whenever there was heavy rain, they became too muddy to travel on at all.

Edward Talbot had this to say about Canadian roads: "As the roads are exceedingly bad in the Summer, the time for travelling in Canada is the Winter. On this account the cold weather is greeted by the Canadians as the delightful period when they can proceed without difficulty to see their friends at a distance, when corn and other produce can be conveyed to the market, when annual supplies from the store-keepers in remote towns can be brought home . . . . As long as the snow lies deep, and the roads are well-beaten, a Canadian "sleigh" passes smoothly along them with great facility and swiftness; and a pair of horses can easily perform a journey of 40 or 50 miles [65–80 kilometres] with a load of a ton weight, over roads that are almost impassable in Summer."

Transportation by water was generally preferred for the shipping of goods from one location to another. The cost of land travel, especially of transporting bulky goods, was much higher than by water. But water travel also had its problems. Improvements had not yet been made to the natural waterways. Ships could not get all the way up the St. Lawrence River because of rapids. To get around the rapids, goods had to be taken off the ships and loaded into boats or canoes. Once the slow, dangerous trip was made past the rapids, ships could be used again. People also

Corduroy roads were constructed by placing logs lengthwise across a path. Imagine how uncomfortable the ride could be on such an uneven surface!

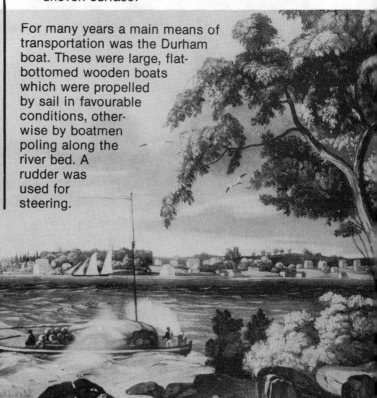

For many years a main means of transportation was the Durham boat. These were large, flat-bottomed wooden boats which were propelled by sail in favourable conditions, otherwise by boatmen poling along the river bed. A rudder was used for steering.

Catherine Parr Traill found coach travelling comfortable. "The coach is so well adapted for the roads over which it passes that I doubt if it could be changed for a more suitable one. This vehicle is calculated to hold nine persons, three back, front, and middle; the middle seat, which swings on broad straps of leather, is by far the easiest, only you are liable to be disturbed when any of the passengers choose to get out."

## FOR DISCOVERY

1. In the early days of Upper Canada, travel was easier in winter than in summer. Why?
2. What improvements had made travel easier by 1840?
3. Would you expect the seasons to have much effect on the ease of travel anywhere in Canada today? If so, where and what effect?

The *Princess Royal* was one of a number of steamboats sailing Lake Ontario by the 1840s. It carried passengers and freight between Kingston and Toronto. Catherine Parr Traill pointed out that, "In addition to their own freight, the steamers generally tow up several other vessels. We had three Durham boats at one time, beside some other small craft attached to us . . ."

had to travel this way, although they usually got out of the boats and travelled on land past the most dangerous sections of the river.

Larger vessels, such as sailing ships, could be used on the Great Lakes, but they could not pass from Lake Erie to Lake Ontario because of Niagara Falls.

By 1840, travel had become considerably easier. Roads had improved and a few had even been macadamized (paved with crushed stone or gravel). Upper Canadians now travelled on land by stage coach and on water by steamboat.

Canals and steamboats helped solve some transportation problems, but distance and winter freeze-up would remain serious hindrances until railways appeared. These would finally make travel comfortable, reliable, quick and comparatively cheap.

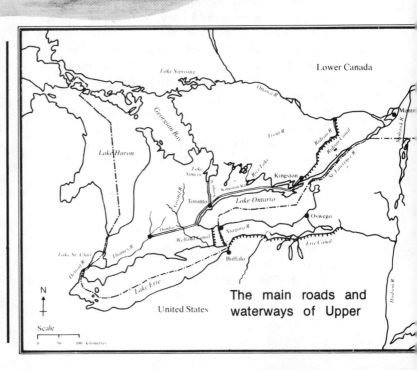

The main roads and waterways of Upper

# Home Life

Early settlers had to build their own houses and barns. Since clearing the land provided an abundance of logs and wood, first houses were usually log cabins—simple and cheap to build, but not very comfortable. There was often just one room and it was usually drafty because it was impossible to keep all the spaces between the logs and around window and door frames filled in. As soon as they could afford to, people began to build better houses of board, brick or stone.

Early houses had huge fireplaces that were used for cooking as well as heating. A great deal of work was involved in obtaining the wood to keep the large fires burning. Unfortunately, a fireplace was not a very efficient or effective way to heat a building.

By 1820, stoves were being manufactured in Upper Canada and gradually replaced fireplaces for both heating and cooking. Lighting was crude—people depended on candles or, in wealthier homes, lamps burning whale oil or lard. Until 1825, window glass had to be imported and so was very expensive. Poorer people, therefore, tended to have few windows or used oiled paper or rags instead of glass.

The pioneers usually made their own furniture. Tables, benches and beds were most often made from pine and painted bright colours. Closets and wardrobes were not common. Clothes were usually hung on pegs on the wall. Better furniture became available as furniture-makers established businesses. Imported furniture would only be found in the finest homes.

Besides the work of building the house and keeping it heated, there were innumerable other household tasks. Every member of a pioneer family was responsible for contributing something to the work of the household. Only the wealthy could expect servants to do their chores for them. Families were often large, so that there would be many people to help.

This house was built by Daniel Stong in 1816 in the simple style typical of Pennsylvania German architecture. The timbers were dressed on two sides and dovetailed at the corners. Spaces between the logs were filled with small pieces of wood and a mortar prepared from straw and clay.

The interior of the Stongs' first home was rustic and the few simple furnishings and utensils are representative of early homes in Upper Canada. The most important feature of the house was the large fireplace.

Daniel Stong's second house was built in 1832. It was a two-storey, seven-room home, built of hand-hewn lumber and covered with clapboard siding.

The interior of the Stongs' second home illustrates the improvements in the family's living conditions. Notice the built-in bake oven beside the fireplace and the panelling covering the walls. After sixteen years of hard work, the family was able to afford certain comforts in their new home.

A warming pan with hot coals might be used in winter to warm the bed in the master bedroom. Notice the handiwork in the quilt on the bed.

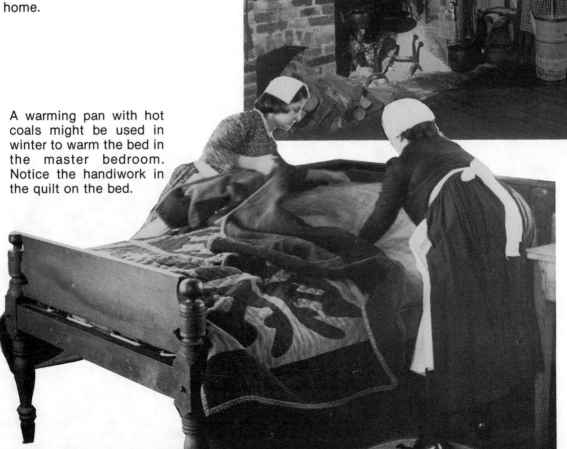

The foods most often eaten were bread, potatoes, pork and corn. If a farm had cows and poultry, milk, cheese and eggs were enjoyed. Occasionally there would be fish or chicken for a meal. Pumpkins, cucumbers, beans, cabbages and other vegetables were eaten fresh in season and were pickled for use during the rest of the year. Fresh meat and fish could be purchased all year by those who could afford it, but most people ate fresh meat only in summer. Salted meat or smoked meat was eaten during the rest of the year.

Everyone in the family contributed to providing and preparing food. The men and boys were responsible for planting, cultivating and harvesting. On a farm, men would butcher livestock and pack the meat into casks or barrels with dry salt or salt water called brine to preserve it. It took hours of hard work to prepare the food required to satisfy the appetites of the hard-working pioneer family, and women and girls were always kept busy. To prepare good food, more than time and patience were required. The housewife needed skills and knowledge—and a little luck always helped.

Cooking and food preparation were only a part of the women's work. A lot of time was spent making cloth and sewing clothing. Cloth was usually made from flax or wool. Women and girls spent long hours spinning, dyeing and weaving. All sewing was done by hand and there were rarely patterns to follow. Women would either copy a design from a picture or old garment or create their own design.

Other household tasks included soap-making, quilting, candle-making, butter-making and sometimes the brewing of beer. As well, there was always cleaning and tidying to be done.

Mealtime was always a busy time. Young girls were expected to help in the preparations. Helping at mealtime, as well as at various other tasks, allowed these girls the opportunity they needed to learn the skills required to run a pioneer houshold. Pioneer women worked extremely hard. In this photo from Upper Canada Village in Morrisburg, Ontario, meal preparation is in full swing.

Nearly all farm families planted and looked after the vegetable and herb kitchen garden. They also spent long hours pickling, preserving and drying the produce of the garden as well as wild fruits and berries for use during the winter.

In the words of Catherine Parr Traill, a married woman coming to Upper Canada "must become skilled in the arts of . . . knitting stockings and mittens and comforters, spinning yarn in the big (spinning) wheel and dyeing the yarn . . . to have manufactured into cloth and coloured flannels, to clothe her husband and children, making clothes for herself, her husband and children;— for there are no tailors . . . in the bush."

## FOR DISCOVERY

1. Describe the interior of a typical early farm house. Draw and label a floor plan for the house.
2. Plan a summer menu for a farm family in Upper Canada. How would a winter menu be different?
3. List the household chores you would have been expected to help with if you were growing up on a pioneer farm. How do these compare with the chores you actually do at home?

Tallow (melted animal fat) was used to make candles. Hot tallow might be poured into candle moulds, or candle wicks were dipped into it over and over again. This was tricky work. The tallow had to be a precise temperature and had to cool at the right rate, or else the candles might crack or not burn properly. The work was also time-consuming because after each dipping, the accumulated tallow had to cool before the wicks could be re-dipped.

The wealthy could pay to have others wash and iron their clothes. In most families, however, the women and girls did these jobs. Washing was done by hand in a tub or by a stream bank.

# Family and Social Life

The pioneer family was the centre of both work and play. Each family member might have many distinct and different responsibilities, yet families also worked as a unit on many tasks on the farm and at home. A family also provided much of its own entertainment during its few hours of free time. In the evening a family might spend time talking, reading or singing together. Wealthier people often played card games and held dances and large dinners.

There was little time for visiting, but pioneers enjoyed getting together for an activity called a "bee." A work party organized to carry out some task that required co-operation, bees provided a welcome opportunity to socialize. In the early days, bees were most commonly held to build houses, barns or mills, chop trees or burn logs, harvest crops. Once a settlement was established, other types of bees were organized: to quilt, sew or build fences. A group of people could get a lot accomplished in one day, and at day's end a dance might be held—a well-earned chance to relax after the work was done. The host and hostess were responsible for feeding their guests, and vast amounts of food and drink would need to be prepared and served.

At times the bees had a less pleasant side. Excessive drinking of alcoholic beverages was a problem. Whisky, hard cider and beer were produced easily at little cost. Whisky was drunk whenever settlers got together at meetings, elections, weddings, funerals and bees. Elections and bees were the occasions when the heaviest drinking and worst disorders took place. Although many people believed that whisky stimulated their energies and helped prevent colds, there were also many who strongly disapproved of the use of alcohol. Campaigns against drinking were led by the clergy, and the first Upper Canadian temperance society was formed in 1828.

Because pioneer families had little spare time and money, their pleasures and entertainments were simple. A farm family might typically spend a quiet Sunday afternoon relaxing and listening to one of the members read from the Bible.

In winter, a family might go sleigh-riding or perhaps skating on a nearby lake or river. In the summer if they had any free time, they might go on a picnic.

21

On Sundays, after the Church service, people often gathered in small groups to exchange news and greetings.

Children's toys would most likely be made at home rather than bought from a store. They would be simple, and would probably include dolls, puppets, balls, sticks and marbles. A hand-carved hobby horse is a toy many pioneer children were likely to have had.

Fraktur is the name given to the old-style penmanship used by Pennsylvania Germans. Fraktur was used to illuminate certificates of significant events such as marriages, births or deaths and was also popular in making book plates, and in the early 1800s it was used to produce valentines. At first school masters or clergymen did the Fraktur work but later artists and scribes would do the work in return for meals or lodging.

22

Care of the sick or injured was most often the responsibility of the family. There were few health care professionals, and so little was known about the causes of disease that even they could do little to cure illnesses. Most towns and rural areas had a resident doctor, but it might be hours or even days before the doctor could come to attend an injured or sick person. In most cases Upper Canadians treated themselves at home with herbs and traditional cures. Pioneers also learned to set broken bones and pull teeth.

A doctor's treatment was often the same as that which people provided themselves. Medical practices were still very crude. More children died young than do now and adult life expectancy was shorter than today.

Corn-husking bees were a chance for boys and girls to enjoy themselves while working. Every time a boy found a red ear of corn, he had permission to kiss the girl next to him! Bees were often followed by an evening of dancing.

Anne Langton

Susanna Moodie

Vivid accounts of daily life in Upper Canada can be found in the books of several women writers of the time. Susanna Moodie is well known for her book *Roughing It In the Bush,* which describes with colour and humour her experiences as a settler in backwoods Upper Canada. Catherine Parr Traill, Mrs. Moodie's sister, also chronicled her life in Upper Canada. Her intention was to give an accurate picture of pioneer life to counteract the sometimes misleading descriptions put out by land companies anxious to attract immigrants. Her book, *The Backwoods of Canada,* is presented in the form of letters from Mrs. Traill to her mother. Anna Brownell Jameson was a noted writer and early feminist. She lived in Upper Canada from 1836 to 1838. When she returned to England, she published *Winter Studies and Summer Rambles in Canada,* a witty account of her experiences. Anne Langton's journals and sketches describing rural life were collected under the title *A Gentlewoman in Upper Canada.*

Catherine Parr Traill

Anna Jameson

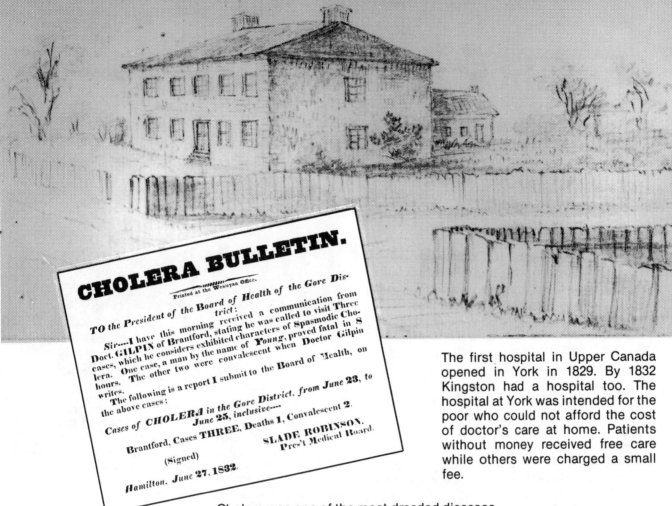

CHOLERA BULLETIN.

Printed at the Wesleyan Office.

TO the President of the Board of Health of the Gore District:

Sir----I have this morning received a communication from Doct. GILPIN of Brantford, stating he was called to visit Three cases, which he considers exhibited characters of Spasmodic Cholera. One case, a man by the name of Young, proved fatal in 8 hours. The other two were convalescent when Doctor Gilpin writes.

The following is a report I submit to the Board of Health, on the above cases:

Cases of CHOLERA in the Gore District, from June 23, to June 25, inclusive----

Brantford, Cases THREE, Deaths 1, Convalescent 2.

(Signed)                          SLADE ROBINSON,
                                  Pres't Medical Board.

Hamilton, June 27, 1832.

The first hospital in Upper Canada opened in York in 1829. By 1832 Kingston had a hospital too. The hospital at York was intended for the poor who could not afford the cost of doctor's care at home. Patients without money received free care while others were charged a small fee.

Cholera was one of the most dreaded diseases of the time. It usually broke out among steerage passengers on immigrant ships and its spread was rapid. Epidemics raged through Upper Canada in 1832 and 1834, killing thousands.

## FOR DISCOVERY

1. What were the advantages of holding a bee to get work done? Were there any disadvantages?
2. Write a journal entry describing how you spent a Sunday in rural Upper Canada in the early 1800s.
3. Why was medical care poor in Upper Canada?

Edward Talbot made this observation: "Gentlemen in Upper Canada appear to be much addicted to drinking. Card-playing, and horse-racing are their principal amusements. In the country parts of the Province, they are in the habit of assembling in parties at the taverns, where they gamble pretty highly and drink very immoderately, seldom returning home without being completely intoxicated." The government's attemps to prohibit the production of spirits were not too successful, and taverns like the Sun Tavern, shown here, did a swift business.

# Churches and Religion

Religion was very important to the early settlers of Upper Canada. The belief was generally accepted that Christianity provided a guide for daily living as well as for public affairs. People wanted church ceremonies for baptism, marriage and funerals; they believed in prayer and the truth of the Bible. They accepted that religion should influence the laws that government made, the schools and what was taught in them, and the rules of society.

The first settlers brought a variety of religious beliefs with them and established different churches from the outset. Protestant churches included: Anglican, Lutheran, Methodist and Presbyterian. Also represented were the Roman Catholic Church and smaller groups such as Mennonites and Quakers.

Freedom of worship was generally respected, although this did not mean there were no problems between the churches. There were often arguments about an established church, about the government's relationship to churches and about the place of religion in schools.

An established church is one that is supported by the government with land and money and has a prominent position in society. It may influence the laws the government makes and usually has some control over education. The Anglican Church claimed this position in Upper Canada as it held this position in Britain, but all other churches opposed its claim.

Nevertheless, the Anglican Church did have special privileges. Most importantly, it received most of the benefits from the sale and lease of clergy reserves. Its position was strengthened by the presence of John Strachan, a prominent Anglican clergyman, on the Executive and Legislative Councils. His influence in government ensured the privileged position of the Anglican Church.

Churches involved themselves openly in politics. The Anglican Church supported the Family Compact, the small group of important people who controlled the government. The other churches supported the Reformers, who opposed the Family Compact. Church privileges became an issue in elections.

In the 1820s and 1830s, the provincial government made plans to share the proceeds of the clergy reserves, and different churches began to receive small amounts of government support. But the Anglican Church retained its privileged position and conflict over this issue continued for a long time.

The Mohawks who came as Loyalists to Upper Canada were Christian converts, and the Governor promised to provide them with a church and a school. The church was built in 1785 and was the first Protestant church in Upper Canada. This sketch of the Mohawk Village shows the church, which can still be seen near Brantford, Ontario. It is now known as Her Majesty's Chapel of the Mohawks.

Methodist circuit rider. The first problem the churches in Upper Canada faced was that of reaching the people. In the early days, the Methodist Church was more successful than most in meeting the desire of pioneers for religious services. Carefully trained Methodist ministers called circuit riders travelled constantly through the backwoods and held meetings wherever people could gather. In this way, the Methodists reached thousands of settlers who were not being served by another church.

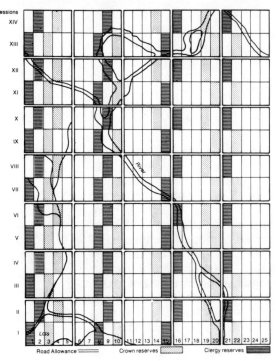

Concessions
XIV
XIII
XII
XI
X
IX
VIII
VII
VI
V
IV
III
II
I
Lots
2 3 5 6 7 8 9 10 11 12 13 14 15 16 17 18 19 20 21 22 23 24 25
Road Allowance ═══    Crown reserves ▦    Clergy reserves ▰

Clergy reserves were lands set aside by authority of the Constitutional Act to support a Protestant clergy. This land represented one seventh of all land in each township of Upper Canada. The Act never specified which church should benefit from these reserves, and bitter conflict resulted between the Anglican Church and all other churches in Upper Canada.

The first church built at Toronto (York) was St. James Anglican Church. It was built in 1807.

In 1812 David Willson, a Quaker minister, broke away from the Society of Friends and with the support of several families, he formed a new religious sect, the Children of Peace. Their Temple at Sharon took seven years to complete and the first service was held in October 1831. The architecture is symbolic: the three tiers represent the Trinity; the structure is square, signifying that the Children of Peace dealt squarely with everyone; the doors on all sides allowed worshippers to enter on equal footing from every direction.

John Strachan was born in Scotland in 1778. He came to Canada in 1799 and five years later was ordained a priest of the Church of England (Anglican Church). He later became archdeacon of York and, in 1838, he was named bishop of the diocese of Toronto. Strachan's central concerns were religion and education, but he realized he would have to play an active role in politics in order to achieve his objectives. A leading figure in the Family Compact, Strachan upheld the right of the Church of England to the total benefits from the clergy reserves.

Egerton Ryerson was editor of the *Christian Guardian,* a newspaper started by the Methodist Church in 1829. In the paper Ryerson urged the government "to do away with all political distinctions on account of religious faith—to remove all ministers of religion from seats and places of political power in the Provincial Government—to grant to the Clergy of all denominations . . . the enjoyment of equal rights and privileges . . . to appropriate the proceeds of the sale of lands heretofore set apart for the support of a Protestant Clergy, to the purposes of general education and various internal improvements." In short, he wanted separation of church and state.

# CHRISTIAN GUARDIAN.

PUBLISHED FOR THE METHODIST EPISCOPAL CHURCH IN CANADA.   E. RYERSON & F. METCALF, EDITORS.

VOL. I.          YORK, SATURDAY, NOVEMBER 21, 1829.          NO. 1.

GUARDIAN OFFICE,
*March-street, north of the New Court House.*

W. J. COATES, PRINTER.

TERMS.—The Christian Guardian is published weekly, on Saturdays, at twelve shillings and six pence, a year, if paid in advance; or fifteen shillings if paid in six months; or seventeen shillings and six pence if not paid before the end of the year, exclusive of postage. Subscriptions paid within one month after receiving the first number will be considered in advance.

All travelling and local preachers of the M. E. Church are authorised to procure Subscribers and forward their names and subscriptions; and to all authorized Agents who shall procure fifteen responsible subscribers, and aid in the collection, &c. one copy will be sent gratis.—The accounts will be kept with the subscribers individually, who alone will be held responsible.

No subscription will be received for less than six months; and no subscriber has a right to discontinue, except at our option, until all arrears are paid.  Agents will be careful to attend to this.

Advertisements inserted at the usual prices—all advertisements for insertion must be handed in before twelve o'clock on the day previous to publication.

All biographies must be accompanied with the authors' names.

All communications, unless they contain £2 or more; or at least five new subscribers must be post paid.

tience with which he endured the scoffs and reproaches of his enemies.  Lead her to his cross; let her view him in the agony of death, and hear his last prayer for his persecutors; *Father, forgive them, for they know not what they do?* When Natural Religion has thus viewed both, ask her, Which is the Prophet of God?  But her answer we have already had, when she saw part of this scene, through the eyes of the centurion, who attended at the cross. By him she spoke, and said—*Truly this man was the Son of God.—Sherlock's Sermons.*

TESTIMONIES IN FAVOR OF THE BIBLE, BY CELEBRA-
TED CHARACTERS.

The celebrated Sir William Jones, at the end of his Bible, wrote the following words: "I have regularly and attentively perused these Holy Scriptures; and am of opinion that this volume (independently of its divine origin) contains more true sublimity, more exquisite beauty, more pure morality, more important history, and finer strains of poetry and eloquence, than can be collected from all other books, in whatever age or language they may have been written.  The unstrained application of them to events which took place long after the publication, is a solid ground for belief that they are genuine productions, and consequently inspired."

on religion as your chief business.  The Bible contains eternal life in it, and religion is the only way for you to become possessed of it."

Dr. Langham upon his death bed, thus addressed the son of a nobleman, who had been under his care—"You see, my young friend, the situation in which I now am.  I have not many days to live, and am happy that you witness the tranquility of my last moments.  But it is not tranquility alone; it is joy and triumph—nay it is complete exultation."— His features brightened, and his voice arose in energy as he spoke.—"And whence," said he, " does this exultation spring?—From that book," said he, pointing to the Bible—"From that blessed book, too much neglected indeed, but which contains invaluable treasures, treasures of bliss and rejoicing, for it makes us certain that this mortal shall put on immortality."  Judge Hale, in a letter to his children, says—"It has been my practice to require you to be frequent in reading the Scriptures, with due observation and understanding, which will make you wise for this world, and that which is to come." And in a letter to his son, he says—"There is no book like the Bible for excellent learning, wisdom and use: it is want of understanding in them who think or speak otherwise."

Lord Rochester, in his last illness, would frequent-

Upper Canada's first Methodist Church was at Adolphustown. This photograph was taken at the centennial celebration for the church in 1892.

**FOR DISCOVERY**

1. Why was the Anglican church so powerful in Upper Canada?
2. What were clergy reserves?
3. Imagine you are a Methodist circuit rider. Describe a day in your life travelling through the backwoods of Upper Canada.
4. Find out about the history of one of the older churches in your community. Write a short essay about the church.

Barbara Heck, known as the Mother of Methodism in North America, was extremely influential in establishing the Methodist Church in Upper Canada. She arrived in Augusta Township in 1785 with other Methodist Loyalists from New York state. Almost immediately they began holding Methodist classes for the early settlers in Upper Canada.

Christ's Church which was moved to Upper Canada Village was built in 1835 in Moulinette for the Anglican congregation there. The altar and pulpit in the church today are from St. John's Church in Stratford Centre.

# Schools and Education

The founding settlers wanted education for their children but widespread services came slowly as there were many problems to overcome. The population was scattered across a large territory so that it was difficult to provide schools close enough to every family that needed one. There were few trained teachers and there were not enough books. More important in delaying school development was the attitude of most people of that time: very few thought that government should provide education for everyone. People tended to look to churches, not government, to provide schooling. In fact, two important leaders in developing Upper Canada's schools were churchmen, the Reverend John Strachan and the Reverend Egerton Ryerson.

The earliest schools in Upper Canada were run by individuals, not by the government. One of the most successful early schoolteachers was John Strachan. He began his first school in Cornwall in 1805 and, after his move to York in 1812, continued this work.

Even as late as 1839, education in backwoods districts might still be provided only by part-time teachers working in their own homes. One such teacher was Anne Langton, who wrote about her work in her journal: "My new pupil is far in advance of the other children. My most distant scholars come twice a week, Mondays and Thursdays; the little ones likewise on Wednesdays, as they are close at hand . . . ." Another entry suggests that she sometimes found her task discouraging: "I go on in a hum-drum old-fashioned way, teaching just reading and writing, and very little else . . . I am quite sensible that the instruction I give goes a very small way indeed towards complete education . . . ."

Early school buildings were simple log cabins with benches for the students and a desk for the teacher. Reading, writing, English grammar, arithmetic and religion were the subjects most frequently taught. In towns where wealthier people lived, Latin, Greek, music and geography might also be offered. This kind of education was not very practical—nor was it meant to be. Practical education or training in a trade or profession was done by apprenticeship. Young people went to work with an experienced person and learned by watching and doing.

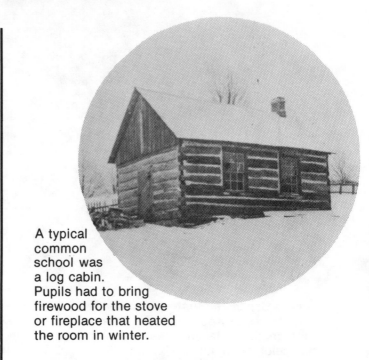

A typical common school was a log cabin. Pupils had to bring firewood for the stove or fireplace that heated the room in winter.

Methods of teaching were very simple and students were often required to memorize parts of books. Schools closed for the summer, and sometimes for as long as six months, because children were needed to help on farms.

Starting in 1807, a public grammar school was provided in each district of Upper Canada. These schools served few children. They were located in towns and charged board and tuition fees which not many people could afford. More schools were needed outside of towns and at lower cost to parents.

Government acts in 1807 for grammar schools (high schools) and in 1816 for common schools (elementary schools) made a start on a public system. Fees still had to be paid, but government funds were provided and the government regulated the course of study, and the choice of textbooks and teachers. The number and quality of schools steadily increased, but by 1841, Upper Canada was still a long way from having a comprehensive public education system.

Meanwhile, churches established their own schools. In 1837, the Methodists opened Upper Canada Academy in Cobourg, renaming it Victoria College in 1841. The Roman Catholics established Regiopolis College and the Presbyterians prepared to open Queen's University. Bishop Strachan wanted to create a provincial university under Anglican control and received a royal charter to do so in 1827. However, strong opposition to his plans delayed the opening of King's College until after 1841. Bitter disputes over the role of the churches in education would continue for a long time.

Upper Canada College was established in 1829 by Sir John Colborne, 1st Baron of Seaton, Lieutenant Governor of Upper Canada at the time. This picture shows the school in 1835.

## TERMS

At Mrs. & the Miss RADCLIFFE'S School, **Niagara.**

**BOARDING** with ordinary Tuition, including English Grammar, Geography with the use of Globes, History Composition, Plain and Ornamental Needlework, &c. &c. &c.                               £6  0  0  Per Quarter

Writing & Ciphering, ... ... ...    "   10  0    "

Day Scholars, (including Writing and Ciphering,) ... ... ...   1  10  0   "

Music, ... ... ... ... ... ... ...   1  10  0   "

Drawing, Velvet Painting, Artificial Flower & Card Work, charged separately.

No entrance money required.

No Pupil taken for any term less than six Months.

A quarters notice, or a quarters payment expected, previous to a pupil's leaving School.

No allowance for temporary absence. Each Lady to bring Bed & Bedding, Towels, Spoons, Knife & Fork, which will be returned.

\*\*\* Bills paid Quarterly.

*Niagara, December 9th. 1828.*

Young ladies and gentlemen of wealthy families often boarded at schools such as the Mrs. and the Miss Radcliffe's school and Upper Canada College.

## UPPER CANADA COLLEGE.

ESTABLISHED AT YORK.

**C**LASSICAL DEPARTMENT.—Principal, the Rev. J. H. Harris, D.D. Late Fellow of Clare Hall, Cambridge.—Vice-Principal, the Rev. T. Phillips, D.D. Of Queen's College, Cambridge.—Masters, the Rev. —— Matthews, M.A. Of Pembroke Hall, Cambridge.—The Rev. W. Boulton, B.A. Of Queen's College, Oxford. MATHEMATICAL DEPARTMENT.—The Rev. C. Dade, M.A. Fellow of Caius' College, Cambridge. French Master.—Monsieur De la Haye.—Drawing Master—Mr. Drury.—Writing Master—Mr. G. A. Barber.—Assistant Writing Master———

Dr. Phillips will be prepared to receive Boarders on the Fourth of January next.

TERMS FOR BOARDERS.

|  | Per Ann. Cur'y. |
|---|---|
| From 6 to 12 years of age, | £35  0  0 |
| Above 12 years of age, | 41  0  0 |

These Terms include Instruction in Divinity; Greek; Latin; French; Writing: Arithmetic; the Mathematics, &c. They also include Pens; Ink; Fire-wood; Washing and Mending.—No extra charges.—Payments to be made Quarterly.

\*\*\* All letters addressed to Dr. Phillips will be immediately attended to.

*York, U. C. Nov.* 18, 1829.

Egerton Ryerson was born in Upper Canada in 1803. He entered the Methodist ministry in 1825 and four years later became editor of the *Christian Guardian,* a newspaper published by the Methodist Church. Ryerson was appointed first principal of the Victoria College in 1841 and was chief superintendent of education for Canada West between 1844 and 1876. During that time he published the *Journal of Education* and was instrumental in establishing a public system of education in the province.

By the 1830s there were church-run colleges in Upper Canada for those who could afford to continue their education, and a medical school was started in York in 1832. There were, however, no law schools. Young men who wanted to be lawyers learned their profession by working as apprentices and then passed exams set by the Law Society of Upper Canada. Destined to become one of the Society's most famous members was John A. Macdonald who achieved his degree in 1836.

From the Upper Canada Gazette
OSGOODE HALL
*Hilary Term, 6th William 4.*

On Saturday the sixth day of February, in this said term of Hilary —
Mr. John Alexander Macdonald was called to the degree of Barrister at Law.

There were very few libraries in Upper Canada before 1841, although wealthy people might have large book collections in their homes. Writing in October 1834 from her home in the woods near Peterborough, Catherine Parr Traill mentioned settlers nearby willingly lent books. Nothing more was available because of travel difficulties: "There is a . . . small circulating library at Cobourg, but they might as well be on the other side of the Atlantic for any access we can have to them."
The first *public* library did not open in Toronto until March of 1884.

**FOR DISCOVERY**
1. Why was it difficult to educate the young people of Upper Canada?
2. Bishop Strachan's and Egerton Ryerson's views on education were different. Choose one of these men and write a speech about his views to be presented at a town meeting in Upper Canada.
3. Imagine you are a student in a grammar school in Upper Canada. Suddenly you are sent ahead in time 150 years. What surprises are in store for you?

The Mechanics' Institute was established in 1830 as a centre for adult education. A library was set up and courses were offered on a variety of subjects including mathematics, architecture and philosophy. Although the teaching programme had some support, the major emphasis at the institute was on developing its library and organizing recreational activities.

# Early Towns

No permanent urban centres existed in Upper Canada before the Loyalists settled there. Urban centres are places where people live close to each other and where they can find services such as stores, government offices, schools and churches. Small centres are called hamlets or villages; larger centres, towns or cities.

From the beginning of settlement in Upper Canada, some people needed or wanted to live in towns rather than on farms separated from other people. The Loyalists founded such communities as Cornwall, Brockville, Kingston and Belleville. Initial inhabitants in the towns of Kingston, Niagara and York were merchants, government officials and soldiers. Later, immigrants increased the populations of these centres.

The location of these early towns explains why they were established and why they tended to grow quickly. All of these communities were located on the banks of rivers or the shores of lakes. Water was the easiest means of travel and the only way to move heavy cargoes such as wheat, ashes and lumber. These sites were also likely to have the water power necessary to run mills.

The establishment of towns and cities brought specific problems. Maintaining safety, sanitation and living standards was difficult. Streets and sidewalks were poorly maintained and accidents were fairly common. Because towns had no regular garbage collection, refuse was commonly thrown into roads or streams and lakes. Many people got their drinking water from these same lakes and rivers. Such unsanitary conditions contributed significantly to the cholera epidemic of 1832. Concern over proper drainage, garbage disposal and pure water grew until the major towns and cities began to acquire water systems in the 1840s.

If you entered Upper Canada by coming up the St. Lawrence, the first community you would have seen was Cornwall. In 1818, an immigrant wrote that it "has a Gaol [public prison], a Court-house, a Roman Catholic Chapel, and a Presbyterian Meeting-house. It contains about 50 houses, and nearly 200 inhabitants, and is the town of Azzize for the Eastern District." This last remark means that court trials for part of eastern Upper Canada were held in Cornwall.

Kingston developed as a British military and naval base for Lake Ontario. For the first forty years of Upper Canada's history it was the largest and most important urban centre. Kingston's large harbour was an ideal place for trans-shipment of goods from Montreal up the St. Lawrence River to Lake Ontario and on to fur-trading ports in the West. Goods from the West and from Upper Canada going downriver were also trans-shipped at Kingston.

Kingston also benefitted from the early settlement of surrounding farmland. Gradually a village formed to provide services for residents. In 1785, a school was opened; a post office followed in 1789. Its merchants sold goods all over Upper Canada and by 1808, a stagecoach route was established between it and Montreal. Due to economic growth in Kingston, the first banks of Upper Canada developed there.

Niagara benefitted from its location at the mouth of the Niagara River as well as from the presence of a British garrison. It had political importance as the first capital of Upper Canada and after that role was lost to York, it became the capital of the Niagara District.

"Queenstown is a neat and flourishing place," wrote one observer in 1807, "distinguished by the beauty and grandeur of its situation. Here all the merchandise and stores for the upper part of the province are landed from the vessels in which they have been conveyed from Kingston, and transported in waggons to Chippawa, a distance of ten miles [14 km], in order to get around the Falls."

Ottawa began as Bytown, named after Colonel John By. He was the commander of the Royal Engineers who surveyed and built the Rideau Canal, and as part of the project, established a village at the Ottawa River end. The population of the village grew from almost nothing in 1826 to 1500 in 1832. Besides handling canal traffic, Bytown served the needs of lumber workers and farmers in the area. In 1855, Bytown was renamed Ottawa and two years later, it became the capital of the Province of Canada.

The main purpose of water systems, however, was to ensure that water was available to fight fires. Volunteer fire departments were established and were helpful, but by the time the volunteers arrived, damage from a blaze could already be substantial. Full-time police forces did not exist. A chief of police called a high constable or high bailiff, and police constables were appointed from among the citizens in the community.

The lure of the city was powerful and populations grew rapidly. Along with the wealthy and middle class (tradespeople and shopkeepers), ever-increasing numbers of poor people were attracted to the cities. Even as early as 1830, there were slum districts, areas of poor housing, in Toronto.

John Bennett came to York in 1801 to be a printer and wrote about it in a letter: "York contains about 100 houses and upwards, and about 7 years ago was an entire wilderness . . . . Settlers are coming in every day from different parts, even from Pennsylvania. There is a road leading from town called Yonge street which is settled for about 30 miles [50 km] up . . . . The country round about . . . is thickly settled—provisions of all kinds (excepting flour) are very dear and scarce and every article is in fact about double what it is in Quebec. York is just emerging from the woods, but bids fair to be a flourishing town . . . ."

York in 1829. The village of York attracted merchants, skilled tradespeople and unskilled workers. By 1812, York had many industries: potasheries, tanneries, breweries, brickyards, shipbuilding yards and a pottery factory. Service industries also grew as increasing numbers of tailors, hairdressers, watchmakers, bakers, teachers, doctors and lawyers were required to meet the needs of a growing population.

The building of canals in upper New York State in the 1820s enabled York merchants to buy directly from European and American sources without going through merchants in Kingston or Montreal. The opening of the Welland Canal joining Lakes Ontario and Erie in 1829 helped York's trade with the West, and as it grew Kingston's began to decline.

By 1834, York was overtaking Kingston as the main urban centre of Upper Canada. That year, it was incorporated as a city and renamed Toronto.

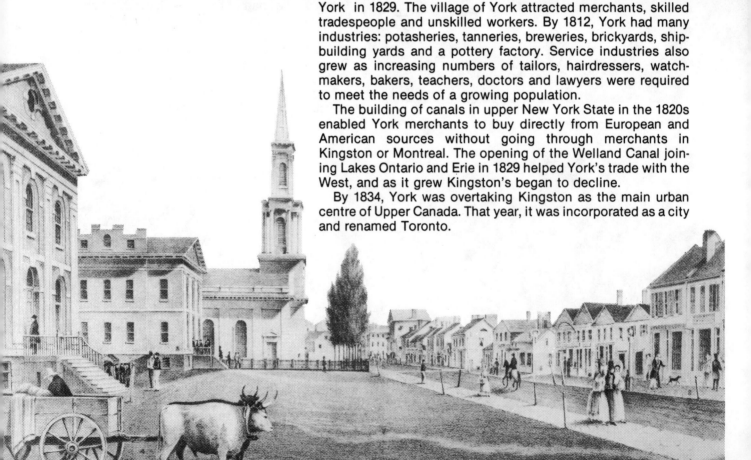

Citizens were lucky if a town had a fire engine, with a tank, pump and hoses mounted on wheels that could be pulled by men or horses to the scene of a blaze.

A family might have a well for drinking water on its property. The risks of drinking polluted water would be less from well water. Still, sanitation standards were very poor.

## FOR DISCOVERY

1. What was the most important factor that influenced the growth of Upper Canada's towns?
2. Find out about the history of your home town. What factor was most important in influencing its growth and development?
3. What specific problems did the establishment of cities and towns create in the early 1800s? What community services available in towns and cities today have helped solve these problems? Are there some that have not been solved?

By 1841, there were many villages and towns in Upper Canada and the population had greatly increased.

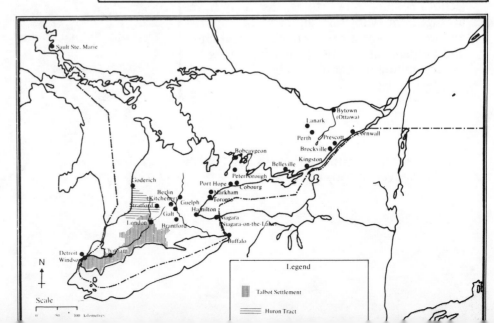

# Industries and Occupations

Most Upper Canadians made their living by farming. Pioneer farming was a complex operation. It involved much more than simply growing crops or raising animals. The tasks of land-clearing and construction could continue for many years before efficient cultivation could begin. While all this was going on, it was quite usual for men and women to perform a number of tasks that in later times came to be done outside the home: making furniture, butchering cattle, producing cloth, soap, candles.

Farmers grew for a market which might be the local army garrison or village, or might be farther away. In 1806, George Heriot wrote that since 1800, "many thousand barrels of flour, quantities of salted beef and pork, butter and cheese, pot-ash, and numbers of live cattle, have annually been conveyed to Lower Canada, upon rafts of timber, containing from five hundred to eight hundred barrels each, and upon scows . . . immense quantities of produce continue to flow every year into the lower province."

One of the first industries in Upper Canada was the lumber industry. Men would cut trees and most of the logs would be used to make rafts which were floated downriver. Some of the wood was taken to sawmills where it was sawn into planks.

There were also merchants and millers in Upper Canada. Men in these occupations arrived with the earliest settlers: Richard Cartwright at Kingston, his partner Robert Hamilton of Queenston, William Allan and Laurent Quetton St. George in York. Merchants, like farmers, usually filled several roles. Besides running retail stores, they may have arranged for wholesale shipment of imports and exports, lent money, bought or sold land and perhaps also served as magistrate, postmaster, militia officer or member of the colony's legislature.

Market at Toronto, 1840. Farmers could come to market to sell what they had produced and to purchase those things they still required or could not produce on their own.

Lumber rafts like this one were used on the Ottawa River as early as 1806.

Grist mills or flour mills were used by local farmers as well as by farmers from many miles away. Their grain would be brought in for grinding and while they waited, farmers could catch up on local news.

Retail shops were run by merchants in town. The shops carried a variety of items required by the citizens of the town and surrounding farms.

The miller was another important person in early communities. Mills powered by water wheels were the most effective way to grind grain into flour (grist mills), saw lumber, and produce cloth by spinning and weaving machines. Farmers brought their produce to the mill and while waiting for it to be processed, had an opportunity to meet and talk to one another. Thus, mills could serve as social centres and often gave the start to a village.

Doctors, dentists, lawyers, shipbuilders, tailors, teachers, printers and journalists were all able to find employment opportunity in Upper Canada.

Early on, craftspeople such as blacksmiths, millers, wheelwrights and wagon-makers were important. As society matured and progressed it provided employment for a growing variety of skilled workers.

Cabinet makers were kept very busy in the towns of Upper Canada. There were many fine furniture makers who copied styles from Britain and elsewhere. Drop-leaf tables, four-poster beds, chests and cupboards began to replace the crude, hand-made furnishings in early homes.

The blacksmith and tinsmith became increasingly busy as populations in villages and towns grew.

## SURGEON DENTIST.

THE Subscriber's Room is at D. BOSTSFORD'S *Ontario House*, where all dental operations will be performed to the satisfaction of the applicant, or no charges will be required. Those who wish his professional services are requested to call soon, as he will remain in Town only a few days. E. A. BIGELOW. 21

York, May 7th 1830.

## FOR DISCOVERY

1. Why was Upper Canada a good place for tradespeople and professionals to work?
2. Who do you think worked harder, the farmers in Upper Canada or the merchants in Upper Canada? Support your opinion.
3. Create four advertisements for your local town newspaper in 1835. Now choose four different things to advertise that are available today that were not available then and write advertisements for these.

STRAYED—On the 14th of last month from the Don Mills, a DARK BRINDLE COW, about nine years old, with two holes bored in the underside of her horns, and a bell about her neck. Any person returning the same will be rewarded for his trouble.

Don Mills, May 3rd, 1830.

The Bank of Upper Canada was the first bank in the province and was established by the Family Compact.

Advertising was popular in newspapers in Upper Canada. The availability of goods and services could be made known to a large number of readers.

CASH will be paid for SHEEP and DEER SKINS free from holes and stain, at the Parchment Manufactory, Dundas Street. F. W. LONG. 23-tf.

York, 7th May 1830.

WANTED a Person of suitable qualifications to take charge of a Free School about to be established in Bellville. Apply to BILLA FLINT, Jun'r.

Bellville, 27th April, 1830.

### LAKE ONTARIO STEAM-BOAT
#### NIAGARA.

THE NIAGARA, Captain John Mosier, commences her regular trips for the season, on SATURDAY, May 1st ; ending on TUESDAY, November 2d.

Leaves Niagara for Prescott every Saturday Morning, at eight o'clock, touching at York, (Cobourg, and Port Hope, wind and weather permitting,) Kingston, and Brockville, and will arrive the following day.

Leaves Prescott for Niagara every Tuesday Evening, after the arrival of the Montreal Stage, touching at Brockville, Kingston, (Cobourg and Port Hope, wind and weather permitting,) and York, and will arrive at Niagara on Friday morning.

#### RATES OF PASSAGE.

| | £ | s | d |
|---|---|---|---|
| To or from Prescott and Niagara | 3 | 10 | 0 |
| From Prescott to York | 2 | 10 | 0 |
| To or from Kingston and Niagara | 2 | 0 | 0 |
| To or from Kingston and York | 2 | 0 | 0 |
| To or from York and Niagara | 0 | 15 | 0 |

From Prescott to Montreal there is a daily line of POST COACHES (Sundays excepted) running in connection with the above Boat.

The NIAGARA (341 tons burthen) is in the best sailing order,—has very superior accommodations,—and her engine, by Ward, is on the low pressure principle.

AGENTS.—At Kingston, Archibald McDonell ; at Queenston, Adam Brown ; at York, Newbigging & Murray ; and at Niagara, W. D. Miller.

Niagara, April 10th 1830. 30-tf.

### NEW LINE OF STAGES AND STEAMBOATS FROM YORK TO PRESCOTT.

THE public are respectfully informed that a line of Stages will run regularly between YORK and the CARRYING PLACE, twice a week, the remainder of the Season, leaving York every MONDAY and THURSDAY morning at 4 o'clock ; passing through the beautiful Townships of Pickering, Whitby, Darlington, and Clarke, and the pleasantly situated Villages of Port Hope, Cobourg, & Colborne, and arriving at the Carrying Place the same evening.

Will leave the Carrying Place every TUESDAY and FRIDAY morning at 4 o'clock and arrive at YORK the same evening.

The above arrangements are in connexion with the Steam-Boat SIR JAMES KEMPT, so that passengers travelling this route will find a pleasant and speedy conveyance between York and Prescott, the road being very much repaired and the line fitted up with good Horses, new Carriages, and careful drivers. Fare through from York to Prescott, £2 10 0., the same as in the Lake Boats. Intermediate distances, £1re as usual. All baggage at the risk of the owner.

N. B. Extras furnished at York, Cobourg, or the Carrying Place, on reasonable terms.

York, June 9th, 1830. WILLIAM WELLER. 30.

and Muscovado Sugar, Coffee, Chocolate, Pepper, Allspice, Ginger, Nutmegs, Cloves, Barley, Rice, Alum, Indigo, Fig Blue, Iron, Steel, Nails, Window Glass, Putty, Paints and Oil ; Stoves, Holloware, Shovels, Spades, Trying pans, Teakettles, Handsaws, Cutlery, &c. &c., with a variety of other articles, TOO NUMEROUS to detail in an advertisement. All of which will be sold EXTREMELY LOW for CASH.

York, Nov. 20th, 1829. 21—tf.

### NOTICE.

R. MULLEN, begs leave to inform the public, that he has received an extensive and general assortment of

#### MEDICINES,

which he offers for sale on reasonable terms, amongst which are some of the latest chemical preparations from London and Paris. Should gentlemen of the Medical profession and veterinary surgeons favor him with their patronage, they may rest assured that he will make liberal deductions.

Hamilton, May 17th, 1830. 30-tf.

### To save is to gain!

THOSE who want bargains in DRY GOODS, GROCERIES, Crockery, Iron-ware, &c. &c. are invited to call at

#### CHEAPSIDE,

King-street, near Yonge-street, to examine the stock now offered for sale, and make a trial of the Goods.

York, Dec. 26th, 1829. PHELAN & LAVERTY. 6

JOHN AND CHRISTOPHER WEBB, Boot and Shoe Makers, Leather Sellers, &c.—Grateful for past favors, return their thanks to those gentlemen of York and its vicinity, who have patronised them since their commencement in business, desire to inform the public, that they have now a quantity of different kinds of

#### EXCELLENT LEATHER,

Bought in New York, and that from their attention and desire to please, they hope still to merit the attention and the portion of the custom of the Public.

York, Church-Street, Feb'y, 13th, 1830. 13-tf.

100 KEGS of RICHMOND TOBACCO for sale by S. BURNHAM.

York, 27th May, 1830. 25-3

CASH will be paid for SHEEP and DEER SKINS free from holes and stain, at the Parchment Manufactory, Dundas Street.

York, 7th May 1830. F. W. LONG. 23-tf.

TAKE NOTICE.—All persons are hereby forbid to trust or harbour Margaret, my wife, on my account, as she has left my bed and board without any just cause of complaint. CALEB R. WHITING.

Trafalgar, 1st April, 1829. 20-tf.

BUILDING LOTS for Sale on the front of Park Lots No. 19 and 20, on Lot Street, and in the Field adjoining Mr. Dunn's, on Lot and Peter Streets. Enquire of Mr. Crookshank or Mr. Mercer.

York, 23rd Februray, 1830.

NOTICE TO TANNERS AN

# Military and Defence

There are two fundamental points to remember about Upper Canada's military defence. The first is that the threat of attack on Upper Canada came from the United States, not from any other country, nor from the native peoples within the region. In communities along the St. Lawrence River and the shores of Lakes Ontario and Erie, there are many reminders of past warfare: Fort Wellington at Prescott, Fort Henry at Kingston, Fort York at Toronto, Fort George at Niagara-on-the-Lake, Fort Erie at Fort Erie and Fort Malden near Amherstburg. These and other fortifications were designed to resist attacks from across the border. The land defences were supported by warships.

The second point is that the principal means for defending Canada were British soldiers and warships. By law all Upper Canadian males 16 to 60 belonged to the militia and were supposed to attend a few days of training every year. They did not always do so, however. And even for those who did attend, it was far too little. Canadian militia and native people did play roles in defence, but their contributions were secondary to those of professional soldiers and sailors.

In 1811, there were about 1500 British regulars stationed in garrisons in Upper Canada. A garrison usually consisted of barracks for the troops, a residence for commanding officers, a battery and block houses. Barracks were buildings where soldiers lived. Block houses might be built of logs or stone and were intended for defensive fighting. In fact, soldiers were often housed in both kinds of buildings and counted themselves lucky because they might have to make do living in barns or tents.

Wherever they were sheltered, soldiers suffered from crowding, poor food, damp, heat in summer, cold in winter and disease. During wartime, they had the additional threats of injury and death. Yet, they fought bravely against American invaders from 1812 to 1814, when the United States declared war on Britain, and Canada became a battleground on land and on sea.

The "militia myth" was the belief that the Canadian militia, rather than the British regulars and the native people, were mainly responsible for saving Upper Canada from American conquest. In reality, throughout the war, the militia would be a significant factor in winning battles on only a few occasions.

Benjamin Milliken served as a private in the York Militia of 1812 and later rose to the rank of major.

The biggest and most expensive defensive work in Upper Canada was not a fort but a canal. The Rideau Canal was built between 1826 and 1832 to provide a water route from Montreal to the towns and cities of Upper Canada which would be well away from the American border. It had stone block houses for defence. Happily, there has not been a war between Canada and the United States since 1814, and the Rideau Canal has never actually been used as a military supply route.

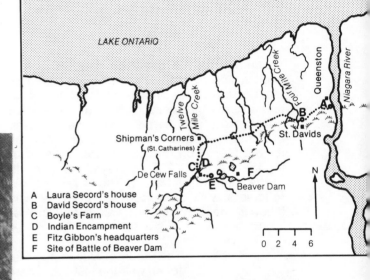

A    Laura Secord's house
B    David Secord's house
C    Boyle's Farm
D    Indian Encampment
E    Fitz Gibbon's headquarters
F    Site of Battle of Beaver Dam

Laura Ingersoll Secord was born in Massachusetts and immigrated to Upper Canada with her father in 1795. In 1812, her husband was wounded at Queenston Heights and she rescued him from the battlefield.

On June 21, 1813, Laura Secord overheard American soldiers in Queenston mention plans for a surprise attack on the British post at Beaver Dam. She set out to warn the British and arrived at the post after walking some 30 kilometres through fields and woods. Her bravery was rewarded—but not until 1860, at which time the Prince of Wales sent her £100 in gold.

Sir Isaac Brock was a soldier who was not afraid to take risks. He believed that attack was the best form of defence and that an officer should lead his men into action, not stand behind them and give orders. Acting on this belief, he won a great victory at Detroit on August 8, 1812, but lost his life at Queenston Heights in October of the same year. For the skill and courage he displayed at Detroit, Brock was granted a knighthood. A monument has been erected at Queenston Heights in his honour.

Most of the land battles of the War of 1812 took place in Upper Canada and important naval clashes occurred on Lakes Ontario and Erie as well as on the St. Lawrence River. The war finally ended in a stalemate, with both the Canadians and the Americans later claiming to have been victorious.

Upper Canada was threatened again in 1837 and 1838, during and after William Lyon Mackenzie's rebellion, by private groups of American citizens who raided across the border. British soldiers were the major defence force then as well.

Canadians have kept alive the memory of the heroes of the War of 1812 such as Brock and Tecumseh, and a heroine, Laura Secord, by erecting plaques and monuments. Battlefields are marked, and every year colourful ceremonies are held in forts that date back to those times.

Tecumseh was a Shawnee chief who had been trying to organize the native tribes of the United States into a vast alliance that could resist the pressure from the American government and settlers who were taking over native people's lands. He and his followers fought on the side of the British during the War of 1812. They played a major role in the capture of Detroit. Tecumseh led his followers with great courage until he was killed in the Battle of the Thames on October 15, 1813.

The Battle of Queenston Heights, in early October, was the last big American attempt to invade Canada in 1812. The British were victorious and this gave a tremendous boost to the morale of the defenders. Yet the price was high as General Isaac Brock had been killed. This drawing shows several stages of the battle as though they were happening at the same time.

On May 5, 1814, a British fleet under Sir James Yeo attacked the American base at Oswego. A landing force of some 1100 men climbed the steep hill and forced the defenders out of the fort. The military installations were dismantled and large quantities of supplies were carried off.

On December 4, 1838, about 135 American invaders crossed the Detroit River and attacked Windsor. The attack was beaten back by soldiers from Fort Malden which was south of Windsor near the mouth of the Detroit River.

## FOR DISCOVERY

1. What were the principal means of defending Canada in the early 1800s?
2. Why did Tecumseh and his followers decide to fight on the British side in 1812?
3. Imagine that you are Laura Secord. In the form of a letter to a friend or a journal entry, describe your feelings as you walked through the woods to warn the British of the planned attack.
4. The Canadian militia today is very different from the militia of 1812. Find out about the militia today and outline some of the differences.

American invaders led by Nils von Schoultz set out to attack Prescott in November of 1838. They landed beside a stone windmill and took up positions there. Fighting continued on and off for four days and finally the Americans had to surrender. The prisoners were tried and 11, including von Schoultz, were executed. It is interesting to note that von Schoultz's attorney was John A. Macdonald.

# Government and Politics

As established by the Constitutional Act of 1791, the government of Upper Canada consisted of four parts: a legislative assembly, a legislative council, an executive council and a lieutenant governor. The legislative assembly was the only part whose members were elected. (The only people who would vote for these members were adult male land-owners.) The governor was an official from Britain, appointed by the British government. He in turn appointed the members of the legislative and executive councils.

Any laws passed by the legislative assembly also had to be passed by the legislative council, and finally to be signed by the lieutenant governor. In making his decisions, the governor listened to the advice of the executive council, many of whose members also sat on the legislative council. Although the elected assembly was supposed to have the power to make laws, its decisions were often overturned by the appointed parts of the government.

At the root of this system lay a belief, shared by the people of the educated upper class, that they alone should hold real power. It was these people who made up the executive and legislative councils. This upper class was a tightly knit group, connected through friendship, marriage, land-ownership and the Anglican Church. It mistrusted the legislative assembly because the assembly attempted to give a political voice to groups such as farmers and labourers.

The upper-class group came to be known as the Family Compact. The assembly members who opposed it became known as the Reformers, while the group within the assembly most opposed to the Family Compact became known as the Radicals. The political arguments between these groups had to do with a number of issues. Among them were the granting and control of land, the organization and financing of the schools, and the power of the Anglican Church. Most important was the issue of "responsible government." Under this system, government ministers would be chosen by the legislative assembly from its own members and not appointed by the lieutenant governor. The governor would have to carry out the decisions of the elected assembly.

The first Parliament of Upper Canada opened at Newark (now Niagara-on-the-Lake) on September 17, 1792 with John Graves Simcoe as lieutenant governor. This painting shows Simcoe receiving a salute from an honour guard of Northumberland Fusiliers outside Navy Hall, his office and residence.

The main battle of the rebellion in Upper Canada was fought near Montgomery's tavern.

William Lyon Mackenzie was born in Scotland in 1795. He came to Canada in 1820 and went into business as a shopkeeper. In 1824 he founded the *Colonial Advocate* at Queenston, near Niagara Falls. He then came to York and soon became the spokesperson for the radical wing of the reform movement. He was elected to the Legislative Assembly in 1828 and played an active role from the outset. In 1831, he was expelled for his outspoken opposition to the government. He was re-elected and expelled five times. In 1834, he was elected the first Mayor of the newly incorporated city of Toronto.

By 1837 Mackenzie had grown tired of waiting for the changes called for by his Reform party. He organized a group of followers and staged a rebellion. It turned out to be a disaster for the rebels, and Mackenzie fled to the United States. He was allowed to return to Canada in 1849. Although re-elected to the Assembly in 1851, he never again had much influence.

The struggle for power developed gradually after 1800 and climaxed in the 1830s. William Lyon Mackenzie, the leader of the Radicals, issued his "Call for Revolution" which began "Brave Canadians! . . . The law says we shall not be taxed without our consent . . . but a wicked and tyrannical government has trampled upon the law—robbed the exchequer—divided the plunder . . . ." In 1837, Mackenzie and a small band of supporters attempted but failed to overthrow the government of Upper Canada. A rebellion in Lower Canada in the same year also failed.

The British government sent Lord Durham to the colony to find out the causes of the rebellions. In his report, Durham concluded that "Upper Canada . . . has long been entirely governed by a party commonly designated . . . as the 'family compact' . . . For a long time this body of men . . . [has] possessed almost all the highest public offices, by means of which . . . it [has] wielded all the powers of government." Durham was critical of the way the Family Compact had governed. "A very considerable portion of the Province has neither roads, post offices, mills, schools, nor churches . . . . [The people's] means of communication with each other, or the chief towns of the Province, are limited and uncertain." In Durham's view, it was not surprising that this situation had led to rebellion. "A monopoly of power so extensive and lasting could not fail . . . to excite envy, create dissatisfaction, and ultimately provoke attack."

Durham's report had a number of recommendations. One recommendation, that Upper and Lower Canada be re-united into a single colony, was acted upon in 1840. The two colonies came to share a single government. What had been Upper Canada became officially known as Canada West, while the former Lower Canada became Canada East. Responsible government, another major recommendation in Durham's report, did not become a reality in the Canadas until 1849.

## FOR DISCOVERY

1. Explain the terms: Family Compact, Reformers, Radicals.
2. What is meant by responsible government?
3. What important changes have taken place in Canadian voting practices? Who is able to vote? How is balloting done? Can you suggest changes to make voting even more fair?
4. Organize a debate on the topic: "Armed rebellion is never justified."

# The Growth of Upper Canada

Change was a constant feature of life in early Upper Canada. Almost every year, there was more of everything: more people, more farms cleared, more mills and taverns, more towns and industries, more churches, more young people going to school. New developments appeared, such as newspapers, steamboats and canals. People could see in their own lifetime difficult pioneer conditions give way to better, easier living conditions.

It was difficult for settlers to keep in touch with family, friends and events in distant places without telephones, telegraph, radios or television. As for sending letters or parcels, "There is not regular Post to Upper Canada from Quebec except 4 Couriers once a month in Winter—in summer letters are trusted to occasional opportunities [given to people who happened to be going up river] . . . . The Courier in winter goes on foot." He took three weeks to travel from Kingston to York to Niagara and back, according to this writer, Lord Selkirk.

Selkirk wrote that account in 1803. Thirty years later, a settler wrote, "We are making rapid advances as to numbers and improvements; when the resources of the country (Upper Canada) are more fully developed . . . there is every reason to look forward to the future with the happiest anticipations from the industry and enterprise of the emigrants. Last July, this township was a wilderness without habitation; there are now upwards of two thousand inhabitants, and houses within every half mile along the road. A village has commenced already; there are seven houses, two of them shops; an hotel, and post-office are in progress—the parsonage was begun last week, and the church will be finished in the Spring."

New settlers expressed a sense of optimism. Catherine Parr Traill arrived with her husband in 1832 and in September, they settled near Peterborough. In this heavily wooded area, they had few neighbours and none of the services they had been used to. With great difficulty, they learned how to pioneer. Two years later, Mrs. Traill wrote, "Very great is the change that a few years have effected in our situation . . . . A village has started up where formerly a thick pine-wood covered the ground; we have now within a short distance of us an excellent saw-mill, a grist-mill, and store, with a large tavern and many good dwellings. A fine timber bridge, on stone piers, was erected last year to connect the

Post Office at Toronto, 1837. An improved postal system meant better communication within Upper Canada and between the colony and Britain and the United States. The number of post offices in Upper Canada increased dramatically between 1800 and 1841.

John George Lambton, 1st Earl of Durham, came to Canada in May of 1838 as Governor General and Lord High Commissioner to British North America. On his arrival, he immediately dismissed the Executive Council and formed a new one. He granted amnesty to all but a few leaders of the rebellion. The British government criticized his actions and Durham resigned towards the end of 1838. It was shortly after his return to England that he prepared his report.

Timber was an important export for Upper Canadians and would continue to be during the Union period. Timber slides such as this one were constructed as detours around the rapids and waterfalls that provided power for sawmills, but presented obstacles to the downstream shipment of log rafts.

## OR DISCOVERY

. What inventions of the early 1800s had an impact on the growth of Upper Canada?

. Explain how one of these inventions affected the everyday life of Upper Canadians.

. By 1840 Upper Canadians had seen great changes in their lifetime. Could they have predicted our society today? What kinds of changes can you predict for the society of the future?

London, 1853, official beginning of the Great Western Railway service. The coming of the railway transformed Canadian society. The benefits of the railway were numerous. It was fast, reliable and could operate all year round. It could carry larger loads than any other form of land transportation and promised to be a powerful new aid in developing Canada, creating jobs and increasing general prosperity.

opposite townships and lessen the distance to and from Peterborough; and though it was unfortunately swept away early last spring . . . a new and more substantial one has risen upon the ruins of the former. . . .

"Canada is the land of hope; here every thing is new; every thing going forward; it is scarcely possible for arts, sciences, agriculture, manufactures, to retrograde [go backward]; they must keep advancing; though in some situations the progress may seem slow, in others they are proportionably rapid."

The hard work and the hope of ordinary people built Upper Canada. This is one of Canada's earliest traditions and all Canadians are heirs of it.

In 1841, Upper Canada was on the threshold of great changes. An era of progress and reform followed, and new political challenges and opportunities were inspired. Railways were being discussed and planned, and they would lead to more rapid population growth, the expansion of cities and the creation of new industries. A foundation was being established for the nation of Canada.

# Selected Further Reading

*The Canadians.* Toronto: Fitzhenry and Whiteside. This series of brief biographies includes the lives of Elizabeth Simcoe, Egerton Ryerson, Joseph Brant, William Lyon Mackenzie, Susanna Moodie and Laura Secord.

Eaton, Sara. *Lady of the Backwoods: A Biography of Catherine Parr Traill.* Toronto: McClelland and Stewart, 1969. A fictionalized account of Mrs. Traill's life.

Grayson, L.M. and Grayson, Paul. *Paddles and Wheels: Everyday Life and Travel in Canada.* Toronto: Oxford, 1974. Transportation in early Canada is presented through a readable text and good illustrations.

Guillet, Edwin, C. *Pioneer Arts and Crafts.* Toronto: University of Toronto Press, 1968. Well-illustrated account of pioneer days and ways.

Minhinnick, Jeanne. *At Home in Upper Canada.* Toronto: Clarke, Irwin, 1970. A profusely illustrated description of the life of the early settlers.

Moodie, Susanna. *Roughing it in the Bush.* Toronto: McClelland and Stewart, 1962. Older readers will enjoy an English gentlewoman's account of the rough Canadians and their unyielding land.

Neering, R. and Garrod, S. *Life of the Loyalists.* Toronto: Fitzhenry and Whiteside, 1975. An excellent and well-illustrated description of pioneer days.

Skeoch, Alan. *United Empire Loyalists and the American Revolution.* Toronto: Grolier Limited, 1982. A lively history of the Loyalists, well written and illustrated.

Traill, Catherine Parr. *The Backwoods of Canada.* Toronto: McClelland and Stewart, 1966. An honest picture of pioneer life in the form of letters from Mrs. Traill to her mother.

Turner, Wesley B. *Life in Upper Canada.* Toronto: Grolier Limited, 1980. A concise history of Upper Canada from its earliest days to the passing of the Act of Union in 1841.

————————. *The War of 1812.* Toronto: Grolier Limited, 1982. A clear and concise presentation of the issues and events surrounding the war.